SEAFORTH IN CAMERA

EARLY PHOTOGRAPHS OF THE DISTRICT
ONCE KNOWN AS LITHERLAND MARSH

•

Jennifer E. Stanistreet

Mark J. Sargant   Andrew E. Lee-Hart

SEFTON
LIBRARIES

Uniform with this volume:
Crosby in Camera: early photographs of Great Crosby & Waterloo

1999
Published by
Sefton Council
Leisure Services Department (Libraries)
Pavilion Buildings, 99-105 Lord Street
Southport PR8 1RH

ISBN 1-874516-05-7

Printed in Great Britain
by
Mitchell & Wright Printers Ltd

INTRODUCTION

This album contains fifty early pictures of Seaforth. The majority pre-date the amalgamation of this community into Crosby Borough in 1937.

The selection has been made from the extensive local history collection at Crosby Library. The breadth of the library's photographic collection owes much to the dedication and expertise of former librarians. Also the generosity of residents (including members of the Crosby & District Historical Society), the 'Crosby Herald' and expatriates, has enriched the collection with postcards, family snaps, topical scenes and local views. The collection, built up over many years, continues to grow. It is a storehouse of the district's visual history - and a freely accessible gateway to local studies.

Inevitably, however, many aspects of life do not figure in this album. The physical conditon of some photographs has prevented reproduction; and the library's collection lacks photographs of certain local buildings, events and personalities. Nonetheless, what follows may serve for many people as an introduction to Seaforth's history; for others it will be a reminder of times past.

In order to assist readers in locating the site or viewpoint of photographs, maps are located on pages 6 and 36. A guide to further reading and a full list of the photographs can be found at the back of the book.

JS/MS/AL-H
February 1999

PREFACE

Seaforth is a young community. For centuries, this stretch of the Mersey shore - part of the ancient manor of Litherland - was known as 'Litherland Marsh'. It was common (uncultivated) land, held by Lord Molyneux, the lord of the manor. The 'marsh' consisted of sandhills (full of rabbit warrens), rough grazing land and the sandy shore itself.

In 1718, by a private agreement between Lord Molyneux and several other men of property in Litherland village, the coastal area was 'enclosed'. It was divided up between these, the new owners, who were then free to do with their land as they chose. They could, for example, 'improve' the soil for crop cultivation, or sell the land at a profit. Lord Molyneux himself gave up the right to receive 'pasturage and herbage' fees and, instead, took one quarter of the newly-enclosed land.

For many years, despite enclosure, the area remained undeveloped. "Baxters" (an inn) is identifiable from about 1747; a bowling green is shown about twenty years later; and a few dwellings appear on other early maps. Sometime around 1810, however, a new chapter opened in the history of Litherland Marsh.

1.

Seaforth House

Sir John Gladstone - merchant, slave-owner and politician - lived in Rodney Street, Liverpool. He decided to build a grand mansion on his land at Litherland Marsh - a lonely, yet healthy, location. His large family (including young William Ewart Gladstone, later to be Prime Minister) plus his servants, moved to their new home. It was set in grounds which covered the area now bounded by Rawson, Gordon and Gladstone Roads. The house itself (seen here in an engraving) was large and square, situated on rising ground within a quarter of a mile of the sea. Sir John called his new home Seaforth House, in honour of his wife's family. The district quickly adopted the name 'Seaforth', and the use of 'Litherland Marsh' eventually declined in use.

Sir John lived at Seaforth House until 1830, when he returned to his native Scotland. For a while, family members stayed on, but from 1835 it was rented out to a succession of wealthy and cultured men. The house was subject to repeated alterations by the Gladstones; but after the 1870s the family failed to engage a tenant and the house became derelict. William Ewart Gladstone sold the estate, and the house was demolished about 1881. Its legacy, however, was an expanding community which still bears its name.

1.
Seaforth House

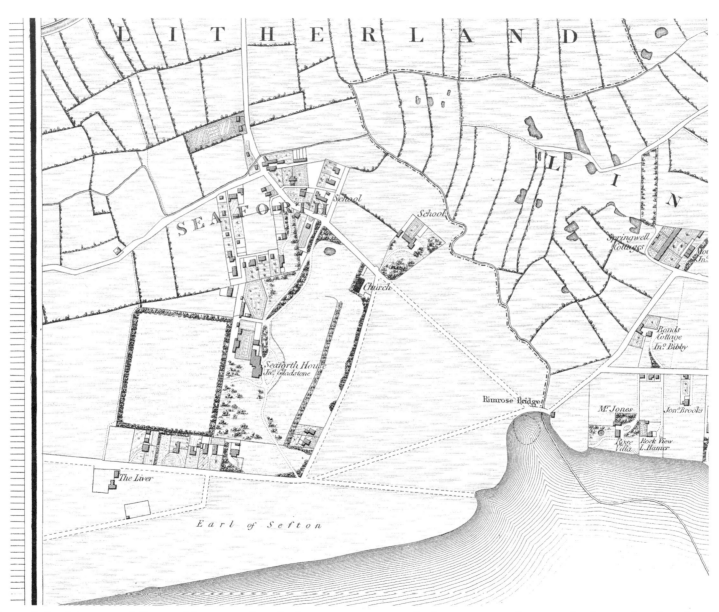

Extract from "A Map of the Town and Port of Liverpool with their Environs including Seacomb, Woodside, Birkenhead, Tranmere, etc. from Actual Survey by Jonathan Bennison, Liverpool, 1835".

Note: the establishment marked as "The Liver" on the shore is not the present-day Liver Hotel at the top of South Road, Waterloo. It may, however, be the site of an inn earlier known as "Baxters".

3.
Crooked Lane

Crooked Lane was said to have been formed originally by cattle meandering among the trees. They were walking between Home Farm - where they were milked - and the stream-side pastures to the east of the Bull Croft (Seaforth Vale). Sir John Gladstone would not have the trees felled in order to straighten the lane. Crooked Lane is now the eastern end of Elm Road, between Bowersdale Park and the Star of the Sea Club. Photo 3, dating probably from the late 19th century, shows the narrow lane between high brick walls. A bowler-hatted man poses on the right; a watchchain stretches across his waistcoat and he is smoking a pipe. In the distance is the silhouette of a policeman, and the shopfront of a fruiterer's in Seaforth Road.

2.
Seaforth Farm

Sir John Gladstone's estate eventually included a Home Farm, a village of cottages, a church and a school. Home Farm, which supplied Seaforth House with vegetables, fruit, dairy produce, poultry and other food, was situated on Seaforth Common, at what became the corner of Gladstone and Thomson Roads. The Common became a focus for village gatherings such as the bonfire on Guy Fawkes' Day. Photo 2 shows the farm buildings prior to demolition in 1937.

St. Thomas' Church, Seaforth.

5.
Parsonage

Having built a church, Sir John Gladstone was obliged to provide a home for the incumbent. Photo 5 shows the first parsonage, which was situated to the east of the church, on land later occupied by Caernarvon Street (later Willow Grove), Conway Street (later Maple Grove) and Beaumaris Street. The church and parsonage cost £4,000 to build. St.Thomas's most famous incumbent was the Reverend William Rawson. He served from late 1815 (when Archdeacon Jones moved to St. Andrew's in Liverpool) to his death in 1872. The Gladstone family paid the parson a salary and extended his clerical duties to that of schoolmaster for their own - and other gentlemen's - sons.

4.
St. Thomas's Church

The Gladstones found that the services and sermons at the parish church in Sefton Village did not suit them, so Sir John built St.Thomas's, in which he could place his own low-church preacher. This, the first place of worship in the district, opened in August 1815. Archdeacon John Jones was the first incumbent.

A white stucco building partly in the Gothic style and with a distinctive octagonal tower, St.Thomas's stood at what is now the junction of Crescent and Church Roads. Originally the organ and choir stalls were in a gallery at the west end. In the body of the church there were high-backed pews and a three-decker pulpit. Pews had to be rented by members of the congregation: these rents were collected by agents of the Gladstone family. A few free pews - for the poorest in the community - were located at the rear of the church. The occupants of these could only be seen when they stood up.

Photo 4 shows St.Thomas's before the opening of the Garden of Rest in 1935. The church was closed in 1976 and demolished in 1980: the former church hall now functions as the parish church.

6.

Seaforth Hall

Manufacturing chemist James Muspratt bought about 20 acres of sandhills on Litherland Marsh at a nominal price. His estate stretched from the Bootle boundary, and alongside the route to Great Crosby - where the grain mill is today. In 1839, Muspratt laid the foundation stone of his mansion, Seaforth Hall. Designed in the classical Greek style by the Liverpool architect and historian, Sir James Picton, the house became a landmark on this lonely coast. Muspratt is known as the 'father' of the alkali industry in Lancashire. In 1823 the family had established a works by the Leeds-Liverpool Canal at Vauxhall Road, Liverpool. Here they manufactured soda by the Leblanc process. Muspratt's son Edmund continued the business, becoming a director of the United Alkali Company, precursor of ICI. The family entertained lavishly at Seaforth Hall, inviting as house guests many famous scientific, theatrical and literary figures of the day. Eventually, part of the estate was compulsorily purchased for railway expansion and the remainder by the Mersey Docks & Harbour Board. Seaforth Hall was demolished in 1924.

7.
Seafield House - Convent School

8. Seafield House - hotel extension

9. Seafield House from the shore

7.8.9.

Seafield House

Originally known as Seafield Hall, this mansion was built about 1860 by the shipping magnate William James Fernie. He was a great bathing enthusiast, taking a daily dip in the sea. After about twenty years he moved away from Seaforth but, with other businessmen, formed the International Marine Hydropathic Company. A six-storey extension (see photo 8) was built on the side of Seafield Hall to create a 250-bedroomed hotel. This Victorian equivalent of a modern-day luxury 'health farm' opened in 1882. The company aimed to attract as guests the wealthy passengers on the transatlantic liners. However, for a variety of reasons - including poor transport to and from Seaforth - the venture (nicknamed 'Fernie's Folly') failed.

From 1884 to 1908 Seafield House was a convent school, the Institute of the Sacred Heart of Mary. The majority of early pupils came from Ireland. The girls originally wore long black overalls, buttoned high at the neck. Later the uniform was a navy dress with white collar; (and a box-pleated gymslip for games). Photo 7 seems to show the girls in dresses. St. Joseph's Teacher Training Centre was added to the Seafield site. Eventually, however, the school moved to Crosby Road North (it is now Sacred Heart RC High School) and the building lay empty. In 1913, when building conversion was underway, it was partially burned down by - allegedly - the Suffragettes. The building lost two storeys in the fire. Photo 9 - taken from the beach - shows (left to right) the lowered extension, the original mansion and the conservatory. Subsequently Seafield House served as a children's asylum; from 1941 to 1947 it was a naval hospital (Captain Johnnie Walker died there in 1944); later it served as government offices. It was eventually demolished in 1970 to make way for the Royal Seaforth Docks.

ELM HOUSE, SEAFORTH.

10. 11.
Elm House

Elm House was one of a group of fine spacious residences on Claremount Place, later Crosby Road South. (See also photo 21) In 1861 Elm House was bought by Peter Stuart, a wealthy shipowner and merchant in the West African trade. He moved to Seaforth from Ditton, near Widnes. Seven years later he added a picture gallery (50' x 25' x 20' high) to the mansion. Works of art on display included paintings by Edwin Long, RA, a known house guest. Peter Stuart studied homeopathy for over forty years. He originally treated animals, then his household, then - as his reputation spread - local residents. Nicknamed the 'Ditton Doctor', he continued after the move to Seaforth. He never charged for the homeopathic treatment, hence could not be prosecuted by the medical authorities. Peter Stuart died in 1888. Elm House was demolished in 1935. The photos show (above) an external view and (below) the billiard room - with art on display.

13.
Potter's Barn

One fine early building still standing in Seaforth is Potter's Barn. William Potter, a wealthy merchant, lived in Everton. From his house he could see across to the Seaforth shore and he dreamed of establishing an estate there. He acquired land in the north of Seaforth, near the sea-bathing village of Waterloo. His first venture was to construct stables and a barn so that, when riding between Everton and Seaforth to supervise the building work, he would be able to accommodate his horse. The design for these outbuildings was said to be copied from La Haye Sainte, the farmhouse on the Waterloo battlefield. Alas for William Potter, his firm collapsed and the rest of his dream was never fulfilled. Today, 'WP' and `1841' are still visible over the barn, silent witnesses to his ambitions.

12.
Barkeley House

An inscription on the back of photo 12 says "Mr. H. Stanley Smith and his eldest son Henry Everard playing clock golf on the lawn at Barkeley House, 1899". This villa was situated near the junction of Crosby Road South and Church Road. As the photo shows, it was a fine bay- windowed house with fancy ironwork and a glazed canopy. The Ordnance Survey map of 1889/91 shows, at the back of the house, ornamental gardens and a fountain. If the photo caption is correct, the house was in its final years for, by 1904, the site was occupied by Barkeley Drive.

This is one example of a photograph taken by the prominent local firm of Foulds and Hibberd. Photographer Thomas Foulds first appears in the Seaforth directory in 1896, at 33 Sandy Road. Two years later Foulds and Hibberd are listed at that address; and the firm can be traced locally until 1939.

Photo 15 is a close-up view of the 'tarry stones' lining the shore. Several horses are being ridden in the sea - perhaps the riders are carters, who are known to have brought their work-horses down for a bath on Sunday mornings. The shore is crowded with onlookers. From Seaforth, families would amble across the sandhills, perhaps to Christ Church in Waterloo, or even beyond. At low tide, children might go crabbing. Seaforth shore was enjoyed by all.

14.
Seaforth Shore

One of the main reasons why wealthy men decided to make their home in Seaforth was the healthy seaside location. As late as 1936 the local council's official guidebook boasted that the area was "highly recommended by physicians". William Ewart Gladstone, thinking back to his childhood at Seaforth House in the early part of the 19th century, recalled extensive rabbit warrens and wide stretches of yellow sand, hard and smooth. He remembered "...the pure dry sands of the Mersey's mouth ... delicious for riding (and) absolute solitude..." Sea-bathing was a local attraction until well into the 20th century. The vista on photo 14, dating from about 1900, shows the lonely shore at high tide. In the distance is the classical Greek-inspired Seaforth Hall, with other mansions beyond.

16.

Aerial view

This fine aerial view of 1932 gives a panorama over Seaforth towards the south-east. In the foreground are the three easily-identifiable parts of Seafield House, with its extensive grounds. Separating those buildings from Waterloo Road (the old sea-side road) is a plantation of trees. Waterloo Road joins Crosby Road South at the International Marine Hotel which stands, isolated, at the apex of a triangle of wasteland, centre right. From that hotel, Shore Road (now blocked off in the dock area) leads down to the River Mersey. Church Road, lined with villas, runs up from the International Hotel towards Star of the Sea RC Church, seen broadside on. Other grand houses at the sea-side, to the right of Shore Road, include Laverock Bank, Sandslands and Portland House. To the left of Seafield House is the sandy beach and, on the extreme left, the sand extends over Waterloo Road as far as Crosby Road South.

Seaforth Barracks

The Battery was manned by soldiers from the Seaforth Barracks in Claremont Road. The barracks were originally built for cavalry. Accommodation consisted of two blocks each for 64 men, quarters for officers and married men, a small hospital and stabling for 80 horses. Later the War Office decided to turn the barracks into a Royal Artillery Depot. Recruits came from northern Ireland & NW England to undergo eight weeks of basic training before moving on. Training was aimed at getting them fit, so as well as parade and drill routines, the men were encouraged to take an active part in sports such as cricket, football and gymnastics.

Photo 18 shows the entrance gates, dated in Queen Victoria's reign 'VR 1882'. A lone mounted soldier is coming out of the barrack square, where another soldier is leaning on a broom. There is a sentry box to be seen through the left archway; while two boys in knee-breeches and ankle boots wait outside the gates. On the left wall a poster announces "Recruits wanted for the militia".

17.

Battery

The shore featured in Britain's defence system - defence against sea-borne invasion. Seaforth Battery was constructed in 1874 on the sea wall at the (then) northernmost end of the Liverpool Docks. It replaced earlier gun batteries nearer the city. Originally housing muzzle-loaders, Seaforth Battery was later armed with breech-loaders. This armament had a maximum range of 2½ miles; it could sweep the Crosby Channel and, on the Wirral side of the river, the Rock Channel. Seaforth was a supplement to the New Brighton Battery on Perch Rock. At the time of construction, the fort was said to be impregnable against direct fire from any ship-board guns. When practice firing was due, local residents were advised to open their windows to minimise blast damage! Seaforth Battery was demolished in 1928/9 during construction of the Gladstone Dock extensions.

20.
Gladstone Dock

The new dock was not, as is often supposed, named after Prime Minister William Ewart Gladstone. The honour goes instead to his second cousin, Robert, who had recently retired as Chairman of the Mersey Docks & Harbour Board, and who had campaigned for a new dock to cater for the transatlantic cruise liners. Photo 20 shows the Cunard Line's "Aquitania" arriving in the dock from the builders on 15th May 1914. At the outbreak of the First World War she was converted into an armed cruiser for the duration. After delays due to the war, German prisoners of war were set to work in 1917 to continue the dock construction, and the work was completed post-war. Gladstone Dock was fully opened in 1927 when, again, the King and Queen visited.

19.
Opening of Gladstone Dock

For many years Hornby Dock in Bootle was the northern limit of Liverpool's dock system. In 1908, however, plans were agreed for new works on the Seaforth boundary, to include the largest entrance lock (120 feet wide) on the river. On 11th July 1913, King George V and Queen Mary visited the area to open the first phase of the Gladstone dock. After embarking at the Pierhead in Liverpool the royal couple sailed down river in SS "Galatea", passing a 'Grand Marine Pageant' of merchant ships, including "Mauretania", "Ceramic" and "Empress of Ireland". A ribbon stretched across the dock entrance was ceremonially broken as the yacht steamed in. The warships HMS "Liverpool" and HMS "Lancaster" fired salutes, and the royal party disembarked. They then drove through Seaforth on their way back to the Earl of Derby's residence, Knowsley Hall, where they were staying. Photo 19 shows SS "Galatea" berthing just after breaking the ribbon.

22.
Seaforth Road

Inland from the Rimrose Bridge, Liverpool Road led to Church Lane. This meandered past St. Thomas's Church to Seaforth Village, the railway station and then on towards Litherland Village. The thoroughfare was tree-lined. Land on either side was sold to wealthy families who built grand houses in spacious grounds. Many shops were then established and, in the late 1860s, the whole road from Rimrose Bridge was re-named Seaforth Road. Photo 22, dating from about 1900, looks west towards the village centre. Outside the shop on the left, a brand of 'famous boots' is advertised; and there are horse-drawn carts and a steam-roller in the distance. Still, however, there is an impression of the earlier - more rural - atmosphere.

21.
Crosby Road South

For centuries, the principal thoroughfare between Liverpool and Formby - and beyond - had been the shore. This route crossed the Rimrose Brook at a bridge, the boundary between Linacre and Litherland. This site is now under the tarmac at the junction of Rimrose Road, Knowsley Road and Crosby Road South. The line of the old northbound shore route now cuts across the Royal Seaforth Docks towards what is still known as Waterloo Road. It was gradually superseded by the route via Great Crosby Village. A proposal in 1838 to turnpike this, and other thoroughfares in Litherland township, was defeated by neighbouring districts: the tolls, they said would cripple them. On the landward side of the road to Crosby, many substantial villas were built in the mid-19th century. Photo 21 shows four such houses: (left to right) Moreland House, York Lodge, Riverslie and Northway House. Only Riverslie has survived, as a rest home, by the flyover.

23.

Sandy Road

In the eastern part of the district, Sandy Lane followed the line of Rimrose Brook from Seaforth Village towards the marshy expanse of the Rimrose Valley. (At one time in Seaforth, Thursdays were known as 'brown water day' because the Litherland tanneries discharged their effluent into the brook). Sandy Lane then turned a right-angle into Little Lane (now Cambridge Road) to rejoin the road to Great Crosby, opposite Potter's Barn. Photo 23 of Sandy Road (as it was later known) was taken in 1937, just before this old property was demolished for council house development. Looking north-west from the corner of Claremont Road, the barracks are on the left. On the right there is a small general shop advertising Colman's Starch, Lifebuoy Toilet Soap, Oxo Cubes and Lyons Tea.

24.
Seaforth Railway Station
The railway line from Southport opened as far as Waterloo in 1848. Known as the 'Shrimpers' Line' or the 'Farmers' Linc', it was extended south to Sandhills in 1850. A station was located at the junction of Marsh Lane (Litherland) and Church Lane (Seaforth). It was originally known as Seaforth Station; the name of the neighbouring district of Litherland was added later. The line was at ground level, so crossing gates kept pedestrians, horse riders and wheeled vehicles off the tracks when the train was due. Only much later was the line raised and a bridge constructed over the road. Photo 24, dating from around 1880, shows a steam engine at the station.

25.26.
Seaforth Sands Station

Seaforth Sands Station was the northern terminus of the Liverpool Overhead Railway - the 'Dockers' Umbrella.' This, the world's first fully-gauged electric railway offered easy, speedy travel along the waterfront, avoiding the crowded narrow streets. The station was situated at the junction of Fort Road and Crosby Road South, opposite the Caradoc public house. It opened in 1894. In January 1901 it could boast the first British escalator provided for public use. However, when the L.O.R. was linked to the main line railway system in 1905, the escalator was removed. (Ladies' long skirts had often caught in the treads, so it had not necessarily been a popular facility!) From a depot near the station, L.O.R. trams ran 2½ miles via Waterloo Five Lamps to Great Crosby Village. This service, which took over from horse omnibuses, lasted from 1900 to the end of 1925; in turn, it was superseded by motor buses. Photo 25 (above) is a view of Seaforth Sands Station, looking down Fort Road; while photo 26 (below) shows the station and a train from the perspective of a crowded beach.

27.28.
Marconi 'School' and Station

In 1903 the Marconi International Communication Company (the 'Marconi School') was set up at Beaconsfield House, 217 Crosby Road South (between Verdi Street and Granville Road). Photo 27 (above) shows this, the first-ever wireless telegraphy school. The Marconi Station, in which messages were transmitted and received, was on the shore at the bottom of Cambridge Road (photo 28). The station came to prominence in 1910, as the link in a murder enquiry centred on 'Dr' Hawley Harvey Crippen. Following suspicions concerning the whereabouts of his wife, Crippen fled the country with his secretary, and sailed to Canada aboard the SS "Montrose". The ship's captain, H.G. Kendall (of Crosby) recognised his passengers from police photographs. He sent a message to Scotland Yard via the Seaforth Marconi Station - apparently, the first time wireless was used to help track a criminal. British police sailed from Liverpool on a faster ship, rendezvoused with the "Montrose", and arrested the couple. Crippen was later tried and executed for the murder of his wife. The Seaforth Wireless Station moved to a site at Seaforth Barracks in 1912 and remained there until 1960.

30.
Rawson Road

Seaforth's rapid growth concentrated more and more houses on to smaller plots of land. Photo 30 of Rawson Road about 1900, shows neat pairs of 3-storey semi-detached houses. These have long since been demolished. The 1891 street directory shows them to have been homes for the families of master mariners, engineers and skilled craftsmen. Looking north, Lathom Avenue and tennis courts are on the left, and Gordon Road is on the right. Only a horse-drawn delivery cart breaks up the emptiness of the wide road.

29
Seaforth Vale

Seaforth expanded rapidly towards the end of the 19th century. However many old, substantial detached villas still stood in the district. Photo 29 shows one such, in Seaforth Vale, captioned 1872. The previous year's census had listed only three houses in the Vale. This particular villa appears to be identifiable on the first Ordnance Survey map of 1849, and even on Bennison's map of 1835. It was situated at the junction of present-day Seaforth Vale West and North. In the photo a narrow road wends its way between the gardens; on the left, in the grounds of an adjacent building, are two greenhouses; and in the foreground are what appear to be fruit trees trained against the brick wall.

32.
Ewart Road

Families have universally taken pride in their houses. Photo 32 shows number 11 Ewart Road - a neat suburban house at the corner of Bedford Place. It was a memento for the Brown family who moved to 71 Molyneux Road, Waterloo, in 1908. Charles Brown (a ship steward) and his wife Mary appear to have lived at 11 Ewart Road from the time it was built, around 1880. The 1891 census records them, their children and two lodgers at this address. The photo clearly shows decorative brickwork, iron railings, a trimmed privet hedge, ornamental gate and - at the windows - lace curtains and Venetian blinds. The site now is under tarmac.

31.
Hicks Road

Photo 31, is taken in Hicks Road, a cul-de-sac off Seaforth Road. It shows another style of old semi-detached housing, which (unlike in the previous photo) can still be seen. Again, the 1891 street directory gives an idea of the residents - engineers, managers and even the chief surveyor to the Mersey Docks and Harbour Board. In this turn-of-the-century photo, some children are posing in the street with their bikes; while the girl on the left wears a fur muffler and a magnificent hat.

33.

Seaforth Village

Seaforth was one of the few Lancashire communities which, in Victorian times, took early steps to attempt reform of its public health provision. Rapidly-expanding districts meant pressure on water, sewerage, and medical facilities; mortality was high, housing was often sub-standard, and the highways little more than mud-tracks. The shore-side villages of Waterloo (in Great Crosby township) and Seaforth (in Litherland township) combined in 1856 to form the Waterloo-with-Seaforth Local Board of Health, population 4,500. Later, this became an Urban District Council, with wider powers. Seaforth Village developed over the years into a bustling shopping area and heart of the community. Photo 33 shows Seaforth Road, before about 1895: the railway bridge is in the distance.

35.
Stella Picture House

The cinema came to Seaforth in 1912 with the conversion of Lathom Hall (the village's social centre) into a 300-seater 'Picture Palace'. This, however, was a short-lived venture, closing about four years later. Photo 35 is taken from the famous street lamp, looking south along Seaforth Road past the chemist on the corner and the elegant bank. Easily spotted is the distinctive white stone-glazed frontage of the much more successful cinema, the Stella Picture House. The Stella, which opened in 1920, cost £36,000 to build. A 'super cinema', capable of seating 1,200 picture-goers, it flourished until well after the Second World War. It eventually closed in 1958; and the Stella Precinct shops now occupy the site.

34.
Seaforth's street lamp

At the junction of Seaforth Road and Sandy Road stood an ornamental street lamp and drinking fountain. This was a focal point for the village, especially at New Year. People would gather round the lamp and sing, perhaps to the accompaniment of the Litherland Silver Band. The lamp was removed after the Second World War. Photo 34, taken in the late 19th century, shows a group of boys wearing caps, knee breeches and boots. The Sandy Road shops stretch into the distance, across the line of modern Princess Way. On the right is a 'hatter and hosier'; on the left, James Moore the butcher has carcasses hanging up outside.

36.

Seaforth Arms Hotel

The Seaforth district had several public houses. In the village itself was the Seaforth Arms Hotel, formerly the Royal Oak. Evidence from the first Ordnance Survey map suggests the original Royal Oak dated from at least the late 1840s. The Seaforth Arms was originally sited - as shown in Photo 36 - at the corner of Seaforth Road and Sandy Road. It was a Threlfall's house; and 'Dunville's Old Irish Whisky' is advertised in the window. In the last decade of the 19th century the Seaforth Arms was moved to its present site at the corner of Hicks Road. The vacated block was then re-developed and a clock was inserted into the corner elevation. (See the chemist's shop in Photo 35. The empty hole for that clock-face is still visible today.)

Church of Our Lady Star of the Sea, Seaforth, Liverpool.

37.

Star of the Sea RC Church and School

Our Lady Star of the Sea Roman Catholic Church began as a mission in 1884 when Bishop O'Reilly invited Father Patrick Murphy, from St. Anthony's, Scotland Road, to found a parish in Seaforth. The first Mass was said in a converted stable, capacity 120, near the site of the current church. Within five years the next priest, Father John Henry Seed, was ministering to 800, and the stable was expanded. A temporary church was built with the new parish school in Seaforth Vale in 1890; then eight years later, Bishop Whiteside laid the foundation stone of the current church. Midnight Mass was celebrated in the uncompleted church at New Year 1900; the following year, it opened.

An elementary school for Star of the Sea RC parish opened in December 1889 in the converted stable. On Palm Sunday 1890 Bishop O'Reilly laid the foundation stone for a new school (and temporary church) in Seaforth Vale. This building - shown in photo 38 - was in sole use as a school from February 1901. It was vacated in 1975 and eventually demolished in 1982.

38.

39.

Henry Leedam's School

In the past a number of private schools - of varying standards - flourished in Seaforth. In 1855, Henry Glazebrook's quirky description of the rail journey from Liverpool to Southport considered Seaforth "...only important as being provided with several human menageries or training establishments for young females." Photo 39 shows the teachers and pupils of Henry Leedam's School for Young Gentlemen, Cambridge House, Cambridge Road. Henry Leedam was the proprietor of this school for many years. It catered for boarding and day pupils, averaging about 150 in the whole establishment. Local businessmen sent their sons to Leedam's: for example Bellamy, fifth son of Peter Stuart of Elm House, was educated there. In his obituary (Crosby Herald 19th April 1924) Leedam was described thus: "A man of sterling character, great modesty, and of the highest integrity, he left his impression on the young lives he trained."

40.

Seaforth Fair

Seaforth Fair was a popular event on the village calendar. Its traditional site was on waste ground near the shore, by the railway line. Photo 40 was taken in 1906 from the railway embankment and looking inland. It shows a crowded fairground with tented booths, caravans, merry-go-rounds and a helter-skelter. The large carousel, which boasted that it was "...patronized by nobility & the elite of the country..." bears the name of the proprietor, J. Wallis. In the far distance, beyond Seaforth Road, can be seen the tower of St. Thomas's Church and the apex of Star of the Sea RC Church.

42.
Bowersdale Park

Seaforth residents could enjoy leisure time in the local parks which were maintained by the Council. Bowersdale Park, off Seaforth Road, is named after a mansion and estate which once stood on the site. (Anthony Bower had been a Liverpool businessman and friend of Peter Stuart of Elm House. Like his friend, he built his own picture gallery.) Bowersdale Park opened in July 1901. Pathways meandered between the flower beds; and an ornamental pond was laid out near the junction of Seaforth Road and Elm Road. The estate's original gateposts - carved 'Bowersdale' - still mark the entrance to the park.

41.
Northern Bowling Club

Seaforth was the home of the original Northern Cricket Club, formed in 1859. The grounds were off Rawson Road. A report in the Liverpool Mercury stated that, following a cricket match against Manchester in 1863, "Dinner was provided in the new pavilion presented by W.J. Fernie Esq. of Seafield Hall". Club amenities included archery for the ladies, and a bowling green. Photo 41, of the gentlemen bowlers, is thought to have been taken before 1879; in that year the club moved to Haigh Road, Waterloo. Subsequently the club found a permanent home in Moor Park, Great Crosby.

Bowersdale Park, Seaforth

RECREATION GROUND, SEAFORTH.

S.S. SCHOOL
TENNIS PLAY

AT SEAFORTH.
U.N.S.

43.44

Seaforth Recreation Ground

At the northern end of the district, William Potter's land passed to a Mr. Bibby, whose tenant farmer grew corn. Later Seaforth Recreation Ground was established here, behind Potter's Barn. Photo 43 shows adults and children - all well wrapped up in coats and hats - in the ornamental gardens. In the distance is public open ground - for decades known as 'Bibby's land' but now part of the docks complex. The houses are at the seaward end of Cambridge Road.

In photo 44, Seaforth Recreation Ground, opposite the Cambridge Road villas, is being used for tennis courts. Taken through mesh fencing, and with a fence-post splitting the vista, the photo shows schoolgirls in their gymslips, dark stockings and boaters enjoying their sport. The girl in the foreground has perhaps taken her eye off the ball to look round at the camera?

46.
Superintendent Cross's Funeral

Seaforth's most famous police officer was Superintendent John Cross. From 1900 until his death in October 1911 he organised winter-time soup kitchens for the poor children of the district. At times of extreme cold, when outdoor work was not possible, hundreds of families might have no income until the weather improved. Superintendent Cross cajoled money and provisions from local businessmen and, with a group of volunteers, provided hot soup, bread and other nourishment daily. In those winters, the number of children being fed per day rose from 280 to over 1200. He also distributed food, fuel and clothing to poor families. Cross's funeral generated a great outpouring of grief in the district and the photo shows part of the funeral procession near the railway station. In 1912 a memorial fountain in Bowersdale Park was erected by public subscription. On it was inscribed: "He was the true friend of all in need or distress". That fountain can still be seen.

45.
Police Station & Palladium Cinema

Law and order in the Seaforth area was maintained by the Lancashire County Constabulary. The local Police Station was in Bridge Road, Litherland. However this was superseded in 1895 by the new Divisional Headquarters in Seaforth Road, opposite St. Thomas's Church Hall. The date-stone can still be seen high up on the building, which now has a commercial use. Next door to the Police Station was the Palladium Cinema - the white stone-fronted building in the centre of photo 45. The Palladium opened in 1913 as a purpose-built cinema seating over 900 people; it closed in 1959. Since then it has been put to a variety of uses, and currently houses a fitness studio.

47.

48. Reading Room

49. Lending Department

47.48.49.
Seaforth Branch Library - `Mayfield'

The original Seaforth Branch Library opened in a house named Mayfield, Bowersdale Park, in March 1906. Waterloo already had a library facility in rooms at the Town Hall in Great George's Road; and Seaforth's needs had been discussed since 1899. At one time, it even looked as though Seaforth might have its own purpose-built library for, in 1903, the Waterloo-with-Seaforth UDC had been offered a grant from the Carnegie organisation. Councillors debated whether to build a branch library at Bowersdale, or to opt for a large central library at Potter's Barn. Instead, in 1908 - to the annoyance of Seaforth residents - the Council used the grant to fund a purpose-built library in Church Road, Waterloo! From the beginning Seaforth's Mayfield branch was too small and, in 1912, it was extended. Photo 47 shows the library, with the Reading Room extension on the right. The Reading Room's interior view (photo 48) includes the notice 'No smoking or spitting permitted'. Photo 49, of a member of staff in the Lending Department, is from the same set, dated 1932.

50.
Seaforth Branch Library 1939

In 1935 a sub-committee of the UDC started to look into the possibility of building - at last - a new branch library for Seaforth. After extensive negotiations, the Mayfield site (plus adjoining land) was decided on. During construction the Lending Department was temporarily housed in Rawson Road Council School, and the Reading Room in Caradoc Mission Hall. In 1937 Seaforth and Waterloo became part of the newly-created Borough of Crosby. Therefore, in April 1939, the new Seaforth Branch Library, Crescent Road, was opened by the Mayor of Crosby, Alderman Herbert Williams. By the late 1970s, a combination of low usage and local government belt-tightening put the facility under pressure. Sadly it closed as a library early in 1980, and has since had a chequered history. It is now known as 'The Crescent Centre' - changed in use from its original purpose, but still valued as part of the Seaforth community.

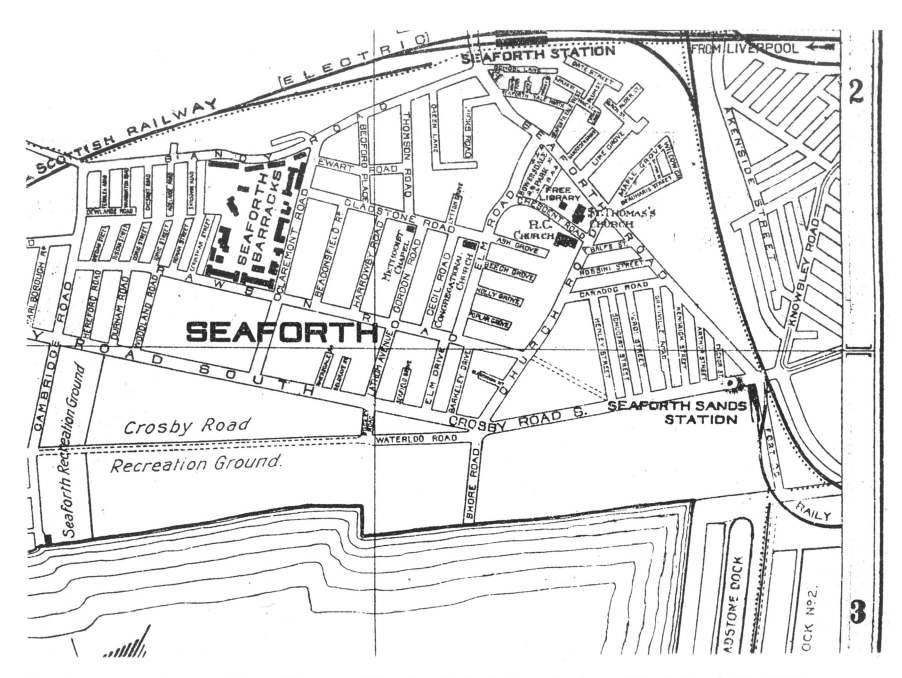

Extract from "A new revised Map and Street Directory of Waterloo, Seaforth, Great Crosby and Blundellsands." (c.1930)

FURTHER READING

This is a representative sample of books and other material relating to the topics covered in the book and to the pre-Second World War history of the Seaforth area. All items listed are available for consultation in the Local History Unit at Crosby Library. Readers may wish to pursue particular lines of enquiry beyond the limitations of this list: Sefton's Local History Librarians would be pleased to advise.

Ackroyd, H. - The Dream Palaces of Liverpool [cinemas] (1987)

Barrow, J.P. - Notes on Seaforth (1960)

Barrow, J.P. - Seafield Hall, Seaforth (1962)

Beardwood, F.C. - History of the Liverpool to Southport Railway (1956)

Bolger, P. - Docker's Umbrella: a history of the Liverpool Overhead Railway (1992)

Bolger, P. - Liverpool Overhead Railway (1997)

Bootle Times 1881 to date (microfilm)

Box, C.E. - Liverpool Overhead Railway (revised A. Jarvis 1984)

Bradhaw, H. - St. Thomas' Church, Seaforth (1950)

Brown, H.G. - I Remember [Seaforth Hall] (193~)

Checkland, S.G. - The Gladstones: a family biography, 1764-1851 (1971)

Crosby Herald 1895 to date (microfilm)

Directories of Waterloo-with-Seaforth (various dates)

Farrer, W. - Victoria History of the County of Lancashire (1911)

Farthing. A. (ed) - Essential History of Seaforth (1993)

Felton, S. - Seaforth, Home of the Merchant Princes: a short social history of Seaforth, part of the Metropolitan Borough of Sefton, from 1815 to 1978 [thesis] (1978)

Finigan, L - The Life of Peter Stuart: the 'Ditton Doctor' (2nd edition 1921)

Forwood, W.B. - Some recollections of a busy life 1840-1910 (1910)

Gahan, J.W. - Seventeen stations to Dingle: the Liverpool Overhead Railway remembered (1982)

Gell, R - Illustrated survey of railway stations between Southport & Liverpool 1848-1986. (1986)

Greatbatch, M.L. - The Muspratt family and the Merseyside Alkali Industry (n.d.)

Hockenhull, N.G. - Waterloo with Seaforth Local Board of Health, the beginning (1955)

Jarvis, A. - Portrait of the Liverpool Overhead Railway (1996)

Lamb, C. - Story of Crosby, Waterloo-with-Seaforth, Litherland & Sefton (1936)

Lanigan, S - Seafield: a tale of two centuries (1970)

McCarron, K. & Jarvis, A. - Give a Dock a Good Name?(1992)

Miller, J.A. - A History of Waterloo-with-Seaforth Public Library, 1895-1937 (n.d.)

National Museums & Galleries on Merseyside & The University of Liverpool - The Liverpool Overhead Railway: papers presented at a research day school (1993)

Parish of Our Lady, Star of the Sea, Seaforth, 1884-1984: centenary booklet. (1984)

Price, D.C. - The Northern Club: history of the Northern Cricket Club 1859-1961 (1985)

Rostron, H.M. - The Liverpool Overhead Railway: a pioneer in rapid transport [paper presented at meeting of the Liverpool Engineering Society, 12th December 1951] (1952)

Quant, H.A. - Notes from a paper entitled 'Seaforth: its history & associations' (1936)

Stanistreet, J.E. - Litherland: an outline history (1987)

Whale, D. - Lost Villages of Liverpool Part 2 (1984)

GUIDE TO THE ILLUSTRATIONS

Where possible, the library's catalogue number is given; some photographs, however, are not yet catalogued. The library welcomes donations of local photographs - street scenes, church groups, school events, village festivals, people at work, etc. Today's picture is tomorrow's archive! For further information contact the local History Unit at Crosby Library, Crosby Road North, Waterloo, Liverpool L22 0LQ. Telephone: **0151 257 6401**.

No.	Cat.	Description
1	-	Seaforth House*
2	BU/STHF1	Seaforth Farm 1937
3	P 20/34	Crooked Lane
4	CH 94	St. Thomas's Church
5	BU/STHR 1	Seaforth Rectory
6	BU/STHH 1	Seaforth Hall
7	-	Seafield House - convent
8	BU/SEAH 2	Seafield House
9	SHR 12	Seaforth shore showing Seafield House
10	PA 10/145	Elm House
11	RD/CROSE 2	Billiard Room, Elm House
12	PA 1/14	Barkeley House
13	PK 100	Potter's Barn: park
14	SHR 11	Seaforth shore at high tide
15	P 13/12	Seaforth shore: tarry stones
16	AE 4	Seaforth: aerial view 1932
17	-	Seaforth Battery
18	AR 2	Seaforth Barracks
19	D 8	Opening of Gladstone Dock 1913
20	D 2	"Aquitania" arriving in Gladstone Dock
21	RD/CROS 3	Crosby Road South
22	RD/SEAR 13	Seaforth Road, looking west
23	RD/SANY 3	Sandy Road
24	-	Seaforth Station
25	T/OR10	Seaforth Sands Station
26	SHR 6	Seaforth Sands Station from the shore
27	RD/CROSM 1	Marconi School, Crosby Road South
28	"	Marconi Station
29	RD/SEAV 1	Seaforth Vale
30	RD/RAW 4	Rawson Road
31	RD/HICS 1	Hicks Road
32	-	11 Ewart Road
33	RD/SEAR 10	Seaforth Road
34	RD/SANY 9	Sandy Road
35	RD/SEAR 5	Seaforth Road showing Stella Picture House
36	RD/SEAR 6	Seaforth Road 'old village'
37	PA 2/14	Our Lady Star of the Sea RC Church
38	SCH/STR 1	Star of the Sea RC School
39	SCH/HL 1	Henry Leedam's School
40	FA 1	Seaforth Fair
41	-	Northern Bowling Club
42	PK 26	Bowersdale Park
43	PA 10/136	Potter's Barn: recreation ground
44	PK 101	Potter's Barn: tennis courts
45	RD/SEAR 1	Seaforth Road
46	P 24/16	Funeral of Superintendent Cross
47	-	Seaforth Library (Mayfield): exterior
48	-	Seaforth Library: reading room
49	-	Seaforth Library: lending department
50	LB 30	Seaforth Branch Library 1939

* Grateful thanks to our colleague, Roger Hull, for the loan of his transparency - it gave a sharper image than the library's print.